Write It Right

Writing a Report

DISCARD

By Cecilia Minden and Kate Roth

Published in the United States of America by
Cherry Lake Publishing
Ann Arbor, Michigan
www.cherrylakepublishing.com

Reading Adviser: Marla Conn MS, Ed., Literacy specialist, Read-Ability, Inc.
Book Designer: Felicia Macheske
Character Illustrator: Carol Herring

Photo Credits: © pikselstock/Shutterstock.com, 5; © wavebreakmedia/Shutterstock.com, 11; © Rido/Shutterstock.com, 19

Graphics Throughout: © simple surface/Shutterstock.com; © Mix3r/Shutterstock.com; © Artefficient/Shutterstock.com; © lemony/Shutterstock.com; © Svetolk/Shutterstock.com; © EV-DA/Shutterstock.com; © briddy/Shutterstock.com; © IreneArt/Shutterstock.com

Library of Congress Cataloging-in-Publication Data

Names: Minden, Cecilia, author. | Roth, Kate, author. | Herring, Carol, illustrator.
Title: Writing a report / By Kate Roth and Cecilia Minden ; Illustrated by
 Carol Herring.
Description: Ann Arbor, Michigan : Cherry Lake Publishing, [2019] | Series:
 Write it right | Includes bibliographical references and index. |
 Audience: K to Grade 3.
Identifiers: LCCN 2018034530| ISBN 9781534142824 (hardcover) | ISBN
 9781534139381 (pbk.) | ISBN 9781534140585 (pdf) | ISBN 9781534141780
 (hosted ebook)
Subjects: LCSH: Report writing—Juvenile literature.
Classification: LCC LB1047.3 .M56 2019 | DDC 372.62/3—dc23
LC record available at https://lccn.loc.gov/2018034530

Cherry Lake Publishing would like to acknowledge the work of The Partnership for 21st Century Skills.
Please visit *www.p21.org* for more information.

Printed in the United States of America
Corporate Graphics

Table of
CONTENTS

CHAPTER ONE

Sharing Information

Your teacher has asked you to write a **report**. Think of something you would like to write about.

You must do **research** to find more information on the **topic** you will be writing about. Your report will organize and explain your research for others to read. It will tell people what you have learned. A report must do three things to inform the reader about your topic. It must:

- Focus on one part of the topic
- Organize the information
- Show the research

What is a topic you would like to share with others?

You can use a report to learn new information
about a topic that interests you.

CHAPTER TWO

Keep It Simple!

A report would be boring if it listed everything about a topic! Instead, you should choose a few main points to write about. Let's say you want to tell your classmates about robots. A **graphic organizer** called a web can help you decide which information to include.

ACTIVITY

Make a Web!

HERE'S WHAT YOU'LL NEED:
- A pencil and paper

INSTRUCTIONS:
1. Choose the topic you will write about in your report.
2. Write the topic in the middle of your paper. Draw a circle around it.
3. Think of six **categories** that deal with your main topic.
4. Write the categories in the space around the main topic. Circle each **subtopic** category and draw a line connecting it to the main topic.
5. Highlight at least two categories that you plan to focus on in your report.

```
          robots in
          restaurants
                │
                ▼
history of              robots in
robots  ──┐             factories
          ▼        ┌──
        Robots ◄───┘
          ▲
robots in │  ┌──┐    robots at
space  ───┘  │  │    home
             ▲  └──►
        how do
        robots
        work?
```

A report about robots might include
information about when they were
invented and how they work.

CHAPTER THREE

Getting Ready to Research

The next step is to **conduct** your research. This is when many writers use a graphic organizer called a KWL chart. KWL stands for "what you **k**now," "what you **w**ant to know," and "what you **l**earned." This chart helps you see where you need to do more research to complete your report.

Make sure information you find on the computer is from a reliable source.

ACTIVITY

Nonfiction Chart

HERE'S WHAT YOU'LL NEED:

- A pencil and paper (or a computer and a printer)

INSTRUCTIONS:

1. Draw a straight line across the top of your paper.
2. Draw two straight lines through your first line, one on either side of the circled topic. They should go all the way to the bottom of the paper. You should now have three columns.
3. Label the first column with a "K," the second with a "W," and the third with an "L."
4. In the first column, write a list of facts you already know about your topic.
5. In the second column, make a list of what you want to learn.
6. The third column is where you will list what you learn. Fill this column in as you conduct your research.

Who Invented Robots and How Do Robots Work?

K	W	L
What I know	What I want to know	What I learned
Robots have been around a long time.	Who invented robots?	
Robots are made of many parts.	What are the basic parts of a robot?	
Robots can move around on ground and water.	How can robots move around on ground and water?	

Keep a list of the sources you used in your research.

CHAPTER FOUR

Find the Facts!

Conduct your research by looking at books, magazines, newspapers, and DVDs that discuss your topic. You can also conduct research online. Be careful! Just because information is on the computer does not mean it is true. Have an adult help you decide which websites to visit.

Write any important facts and **statistics** you find on note cards. Also mention where you found your information. Make sure you do not simply copy what other people have said. You can either state information a different way or explain that you are **quoting** someone else.

Research Your Topic!

HERE'S WHAT YOU'LL NEED:

- Books, magazines, newspapers, DVDs, and access to the internet
- A pencil
- Note cards

INSTRUCTIONS:

1. Gather your research materials.
2. Write each new fact and statistic you find on a note card.
3. On the bottom of each card, record where you found the information.

Sample Research Note Card

Book: *Robots*

Author: Josh Gregory

"During the 1960s, inventor George Devol designed and built a robotic arm called the Unimate. This groundbreaking creation changed the world of robots forever."

Next, you must decide what information to use from your research. Go back to your KWL chart. Filling in the chart will help you organize your facts and statistics.

ACTIVITY

Organize Your Information!

HERE'S WHAT YOU'LL NEED:
- Note cards
- Your KWL chart
- A pencil

INSTRUCTIONS:

1. Reread the information you collected on your note cards.

2. Write down each fact or statistic in the "L" column. These will answer the questions in the "W" column.

Who Invented Robots and How Do Robots Work?

K	W	L
What I know	What I want to know	What I learned
Robots have been around a long time.	Who invented robots?	The first working robot was created by inventor George Devol.
Robots are made of many parts.	What are the basic parts of a robot?	A computer, sensors, and actuators
Robots can move around on ground and water.	How can robots move around on ground and water?	Robots move using tracks, wheels, or legs.

CHAPTER FIVE

The Final Report

It is time to write your report! Begin by writing an opening paragraph that explains the main topic. Get your reader's attention. A question is a good way to begin. You may also share a quote or an interesting statistic.

The **body** of your report comes after the opening. Write a paragraph for each of the categories you researched. Include a **heading** for each topic to let readers know what is coming next. Use your KWL chart to decide which information to include in the body.

Wrap everything up by restating the main idea of your report. At the end of your report, include a picture that supports your topic. A map or diagram can be helpful. Now the only thing your report needs is a title. The title should state the topic of your report.

Organize Your Information!

HERE'S WHAT YOU'LL NEED:

- Your KWL chart
- A pencil and paper (or computer and printer)

INSTRUCTIONS:

1. Write an opening paragraph.

2. Write a paragraph for each category in the body of your report. Remember to include headings!

3. Write an ending statement. Give your report a title.

Facts About Robots

You may have seen robots in a movie or on TV. But what do you know about who invented robots or how they are made? This report will help to answer those questions.

The First Robots

Robots have been working since 1961. George Devol was an inventor. He created a robotic arm called a Unimate. General Motors began using the Unimate to assemble cars. Devol's invention forever changed the world of robotics! I learned this from a book titled *Robots* by Josh Gregory.

Parts of a Robot

All robots have three main parts: a computer, sensors, and actuators. The computer is the robot's brain. It is programmed to do certain tasks. The sensors are like your five senses. They help the robot see, hear, smell, and touch. The actuators receive messages from the computer. This directs movements, voice, and more.

How Do Robots Move?

Some robots are programmed to do one job over and over. Robots that move use legs, tracks, or wheels. Robots with legs can step over objects. This is helpful after a hurricane when power lines have fallen across the road. Robots on tracks are used on rough ground such as hot deserts. Robots on wheels can move fast. One robot on wheels can vacuum your home!

Now you know a little more about robots. They are a lot like humans, but they can only do what they have been programmed to do.

Unusual details will hold your readers' attention.

CHAPTER SIX

Reread Your Writing

Don't forget to check your report for any grammar or spelling mistakes. Will you read your report to your class or hang it somewhere in the classroom? Everyone will enjoy finding out all that you have learned!

Ask another person to read your report to give you feedback and check for mistakes.

Do a Final Check!

Ask yourself these questions as you reread your report:

- Do I report on one main topic?

- Do I mention at least two categories that deal with my topic?

- Do I use my research to explain what I learned?

- Do I include a title in my report?

- Do I organize my information into an opening, a body, and a closing?

- Do I have a heading for each of the paragraphs in the body?

- Do I use correct grammar and spelling?

GLOSSARY

body (BAH-dee) the main part of a report

categories (KAT-ih-gor-eez) ideas within a main topic

conduct (kuhn-DUHKT) carry out

graphic organizer (GRAF-ik OR-guh-nize-ur) a drawing that helps organize ideas

heading (HED-ing) the title of a paragraph

quoting (KWOTE-ing) repeating someone's exact words

report (rih-PORT) a writing project that shares information about a certain topic

research (REE-surch) the act of collecting information about a topic

statistics (stuh-TIS-tiks) a collection of numbers that deal with a certain topic

subtopic (SUHB-tah-pik) a subject that is part of a broader topic

topic (TAH-pik) subject

BOOKS

Bentley, Nancy. *Don't Be a Copycat! Write a Great Report Without Plagiarizing.* Berkeley Heights, NJ: Enslow Publishers, 2008.

Herman, Gail. *Make-a-Splash Writing Rules.* Pleasantville, NY: Gareth Stevens Publishers, 2010.

WEBSITES

Scholastic: Write a Winning Research Report
*https://www.scholastic.com/parents/school-success/homework-help/homework-project-tips/write-winning-research-report.ht*ml
Discover more tips for writing great research reports.

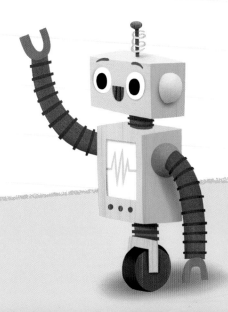

INDEX

About the AUTHORS

Cecilia Minden is the former director of the Language and Literacy Program at Harvard Graduate School of Education. She earned her doctorate from the University of Virginia. While at Harvard, Dr. Minden also taught several writing courses. Her research focused on early literacy skills and developing phonics curriculums. She is now a literacy consultant and the author of over 100 books for children. Dr. Minden lives with her family in McKinney, Texas. She enjoys helping students become interested in reading and writing.

Kate Roth has a doctorate from Harvard University in language and literacy and a master's degree from Columbia University Teachers College in curriculum and teaching. Her work focuses on writing instruction in the primary grades. She has taught kindergarten, first grade, and Reading Recovery. She has also instructed hundreds of teachers from around the world in early literacy practices. She lived with her husband and three children in China for many years, and now they live in Connecticut.